IN HIS EYES

Becoming the Woman God Made You to Be

MARGARET FEINBERG

THOMAS NELSON
Since 1798

NASHVILLE   DALLAS   MEXICO CITY   RIO DE JANEIRO

Published in Nashville, Tennessee, by Thomas Nelson. Thomas Nelson is a trademark of Thomas Nelson, Inc.

Thomas Nelson, Inc., titles may be purchased in bulk for educational, business, fund-raising, or sales promotional use. For information, please e-mail SpecialMarkets@ ThomasNelson.com.

All Scripture quotations are taken from the New King James Version. © 1982 by Thomas Nelson, Inc. Used by permission. All rights reserved.

Page design: Crosslin Creative

978-0-529-12300-8

Printed in the United States of America

13 14 15 16 17 QG 5 4 3 2 1

Contents

Introduction

The Biggest Question

"Being confident of this very thing, that He who has begun a good work in you will complete *it* until the day of Jesus Christ."

Philippians 1:6

Everyone wakes up with at least one big question each day. Some of the most common questions we ask ourselves as we reach for the snooze alarm may include, "Is it morning already?" "Can't I sleep a little longer?" and "Where's the coffee?"

But the biggest question we ask each day isn't about catching more shut-eye or starting a pot of coffee. This question runs deeper and, at times, is a lot harder to identify. The biggest question is something that lurks in the back of our minds, affecting our attitude, outlook, and behavior. When we're really honest, our biggest question probably sounds something like this:

"Am I really loved?" "Why am I here?" "Does what I do matter?" "Do I matter?" or "Do I really belong?"

While the biggest question differs for each of us based on our background, personality, and stage in life, most of us spend a lot of time and energy searching for an answer even if we never say the question out loud. For example, though we may not ask someone, "Am I really loved?" we may look for people to show us affection and approval throughout the day. Though we may not ask our co-workers or friends, "Does what I do matter?" we may look for every opportunity to earn a special award, a boss's recognition, or another promotion. Though we may not ask fellow church or family members, "Do I really belong?" we may find ourselves second-guessing how we handled ourselves or responded to someone after a gathering.

No matter what big question we're facing, only One can provide the answer that satisfies the deepest parts of our souls. The Creator of the universe alone holds the answer to your biggest questions. God wants to answer the questions, "Am I really loved?" "Does what I do matter?" "Do I really belong?" and every other big question you may be facing, with the resounding message of His love.

Rather than turn to others to answer our biggest questions, we can choose to go to God. And when we do, we find God embracing us—the deepest and most hidden parts of us—and loving us more than we ever thought possible.

My hope and prayer is that through this study you'll not only recognize the biggest question you're asking in this season of life, but that you'll courageously take that question to God. And when you do, you'll discover an answer through the Scripture that infuses you with God's love, grace, kindness, peace, and joy.

Blessings,
Margaret Feinberg

What We Believe Shapes Who We Become

People talk a lot about waking up on the wrong side of the bed, but when was the last time you woke up on the right side of the bed? When was the last time you told yourself you were going to have a great day—and you did? The way we think and what we believe affect everything from our outlook to our attitude and actions. This is especially true when it comes to our faith. Maybe this is one reason God goes to great lengths throughout the Bible to say some pretty amazing things about who we are in Him.

"In Him we have redemption through His blood, the forgiveness of sins, according to the riches of His grace which He made to abound toward us in all wisdom and prudence."

Ephesians 1:7–8

Wholly Forgiven by God

Forgiveness is one of the greatest gifts God gives us. A friend of mine once stumbled on a sign that read:

> If we had needed healing, God would have sent a Physician.
> If we had needed knowledge, God would have sent an
>   Educator.
> If we had needed information, God would have sent a Scientist.
> If we had needed money, God would have sent a Banker.
> Because we needed forgiveness, God sent a Savior.

This wondrous gift of forgiveness is extended to us through Jesus Christ and the sacrifice He made on the cross. Through Jesus' death and resurrection, everything that stood between you and God is erased forever and ever. You are forgiven.

But what does being forgiven and extending forgiveness to others really mean?

Forgiveness is granting pardon or giving up all claims of something owed. Forgiveness means wiping the slate clean and cancelling any indebtedness.

Consider the following modern-day example. A bank named the Crédit Municipal de Paris practiced forgiveness in a practical fashion. They've been offering affordable and accessible loans to the residents of Paris since 1637. To celebrate their 375th anniversary, the Crédit Municipal de Paris cancelled debts of the city's poorest. More than thirty-five hundred people had their slates wiped clean. They could begin again.

While the grace and forgiveness extended at the Crédit Municipal de Paris is noteworthy, God's forgiveness extends beyond our wildest imaginations. God's Son stepped in and took the weight of our sins on Himself. Jesus died on the cross, bridging the gap between broken humanity and a perfect God. All debts were paid. Every last cent. Forever and ever!

Through Christ, God wholly forgives us. Psalm 103:12 reminds us, "As far as the east is from the west, *so* far has He removed our transgressions from us." This means when God looks at you, He no longer sees a list of wrongdoings or sins you've committed, but instead treasures you as holy and blameless.

God not only freely offers complete forgiveness but challenges us to humble our hearts and completely forgive those around us. Only then can we truly experience the freedom that walks hand in hand with forgiveness.

Jesus died on the cross, bridging the gap between broken humanity and a perfect God.

1. On the continuum below, mark how easy experiencing God's forgiveness is for you. Then explain your response.

●————————————————————————————————————●

**I experience God's
forgiveness wholly and
completely with ease.**

**I struggle to
accept and feel
God's forgiveness.**

2. When receiving God's forgiveness, we need to ground ourselves in what the Bible says. Look up the following passages. Record what each passage reveals about God's forgiveness.

   Psalm 86:4–5:

   Psalm 103:8–12:

   Isaiah 1:18:

   Isaiah 38:17:

3. Which of the passages you looked up is most meaningful to you? Why?

God extends radical forgiveness to us. Though we may tell ourselves that God can't possibly forgive us, God can remove any and all sin from our lives through Christ. The Bible uses rich imagery to show how God responds to our sins.

4. Using the chart below, draw a line between the biblical passage and the image of forgiveness to which it alludes. Then circle the verbs describing how God responds to our sins.

Scripture	Forgiveness is . . .
Psalm 51:9	God covering our sins.
Colossians 2:13	God throwing our sins into the deepest sea.
Psalm 32:1	God making us alive together with Him.
Micah 7:19	God hiding His face from our sins.

5. Which image of how God responds to sin from the chart above fills you with the most gratitude? Why?

Despite God's readiness to forgive us, sometimes we don't feel ready to forgive others. At times, forgiveness isn't just hard, but can feel downright impossible. Yet God's call to forgive remains.

6. **Read Mark 11:25**. What are three specific situations in your life where you're struggling to extend forgiveness? (Hint: Think of people you don't want to run into at the supermarket or phone calls you try to avoid.)

✤ _____

✤ _____

✤ _____

When facing these situations, it is important to remember we're wholly forgiven and to specifically remember how and when God has shown us forgiveness.

7. In the space below, make a list of ten specific things for which God has forgiven you. How does remembering how God has forgiven you prepare your heart for forgiving others?

✠ _____

✠ _____

✠ _____

✠ _____

✠ _____

✠ _____

✠ _____

✠ _____

✠ _____

✠ _____

8. **Read 2 Corinthians 5:18–19.** In what ways are you being challenged to forgive others and become a minister of reconciliation right now?

As you close your study in this chapter, reflect again on the three specific situations in your life where you're struggling to extend forgiveness. Spend some time asking God for His strength and grace to forgive each person. Then boldly take the step and choose to forgive.

> You are wholly forgiven by God. The slate has been completely wiped clean. Remembering how much God has forgiven you will strengthen you to extend forgiveness to others.

Digging Deeper

Read Matthew 18:23–35. In this story, Jesus told of a servant who owed the king an impossible amount of money. When pardoned from the debt, the servant turned around and threw another man in jail for a far smaller debt owed. Just as God forgives us, we are called to extend forgiveness to those around us—no matter the debt. When in your life have you behaved like the forgiving king? When in your life have you behaved like the unmerciful servant?

✤ Personal Challenge

Pick up a journal or sheet of paper, and spend ten minutes asking God to bring to mind any people you need to forgive. Over the next week, prayerfully consider how to forgive those listed and erase the debt for whatever wrong they may have done to you. Continue to pray for each person listed every day this week and ask for God's blessing on their lives.

"The Spirit Himself bears witness with our spirit that we are children of God."

Romans 8:16

Wondrous Children of God

You are a child of the Creator of the universe. Think about this miracle for a moment: God calls you His own!

In the gospel of John, a religious leader by the name of Nicodemus approached Jesus. He was struggling to wrap his mind around Jesus' identity. Jesus responded by telling Nicodemus that unless he was born again, he couldn't see the kingdom of God (John 3:3).

"Born again" may seem like a strange phrase, but when a person is born into this world, she enters as a child. When a person accepts Christ as her Savior, she is born again, becoming a child of God. In essence, she's reborn, or "born again," since God gives her entrance or birth into this new life of following Jesus. When we choose to become followers of Jesus, we become God's kids.

God identifies Himself as our Father. As His children, we can call on God anytime—24/7—knowing He is more than ready to respond. Our heavenly Father is not unapproachable, but near to us. We can approach our Father with the confidence that

He wants to spend time with and listen to us. Unlike earthly parents, our heavenly Father is perfect. He loves us unconditionally and takes responsibility to care for us. Now this doesn't mean we won't face hardship or illness, but rather, in those moments, God remains with us and provides the grace we need.

At times, our infinitely patient and profoundly wise Father will need to discipline us. But even when we experience discipline, we can rest assured it's for our good, producing long-lasting fruit of righteousness and goodness in our lives.

Being children of God also means we can expect an inheritance from our Father. All the property of our heavenly Father, all the spiritual riches in Christ, which are both in this present life and in the life to come, are available to us. We are heirs of God. And throughout this life we experience gifts of God—joy, strength, peace, salvation, hope, and more—that we can share with others.

As children of God, we are given an abundant future.

As wondrous children of God, we also experience changes in our relationships with other people. Those who also choose to follow Jesus are now our brothers and sisters. They may be much younger or older, they may live in our neighborhoods or in another country, they may speak our language or a distant dialect, but together we are part of God's family. We are able to have fellowship with God and each other.

As children of God, we are given an abundant future. This life and this world are not the end of the story; they are only the beginning. We are destined for heaven. In John 14:2, Jesus said His Father's house has many rooms and promised to prepare a place for us. Those who choose to believe in Christ will live together in heaven for all eternity.

The God of the universe loves us so much that He wants us to know Him as Father, receive an eternal heritance, become part of His family, and enjoy Him forever. Indeed, being called children of God is wondrous.

1. What does being a child of God mean to you? In the space below, write out your definition of what a "child of God" means.

Throughout Jesus' teachings, He regularly referred to God as "Abba" or Father. In the Sermon on the Mount (Matthew 5–7), Jesus used the term "Father" to refer to God—reminding His listeners that God is both His Father and our Father.

2. Read the following passage aloud and circle each time the word "Father" is used as the name of God.

> Take heed that you do not do your charitable deeds before men, to be seen by them. Otherwise you have no reward from your Father in heaven. Therefore, when you do a charitable deed, do not sound a trumpet before you as the hypocrites do in the synagogues and in the streets, that they may have glory from men. Assuredly, I say to you, they have their reward. But when you do a charitable deed, do not let your left hand know what your right hand is doing, that your charitable deed may be in secret; and your Father who sees in secret will Himself reward you openly.

And when you pray, you shall not be like the hypocrites. For they love to pray standing in the synagogues and on the corners of the streets, that they may be seen by men. Assuredly, I say to you, they have their reward. But you, when you pray, go into your room, and when you have shut your door, pray to your Father who *is* in the secret *place*; and your Father who sees in secret will reward you openly. And when you pray, do not use vain repetitions as the heathen *do*. For they think that they will be heard for their many words. (Matthew 6:1–7)

How does recognizing God as Father affect your understanding of Jesus' teaching?

Of all the followers of Jesus, the disciple John laid hold of the love of God to such an extent that it infused all his writings. The love of God is highlighted throughout the gospel of John, 1 John, 2 John, 3 John, as well as the book of Revelation.

3. **Read Psalm 103:13 and 1 John 3:1–3**. What images or words come to your mind when you think of God as your Father? In what areas of your life do you most want to become like your heavenly Father right now?

4. **Read Matthew 6:26–34**. What do Jesus' words reveal about God's desire to care for us? What prevents you from trusting God as your Father who wants to provide for you?

Since we are God's children, our Father doesn't just want to provide for us, but He also wants to give us an inheritance.

5. Look up each of the following passages. What does each one reveal about our inheritance in Christ?

John 14:1–3:

Romans 8:16–17:

Galatians 4:4–7:

Ephesians 1:3–14:

Titus 3:5–7:

How have you experienced the inheritance God promises you?

Being a child of God means you have brothers and sisters around the globe. Christianity is so far-spread and wide-reaching no specific region can claim to be a center of global Christianity. You are part of a two-billion-plus person family that is still growing. From the CEO of a major company, to the neighbor down the street, to orphans in a remote African village, our brothers and sisters in Christ live everywhere.

6. **Read Galatians 6:10**. What opportunities have you had in the past month to show kindness and generosity to your brothers and sisters in Christ? When in the past month have you experienced kindness and generosity from your brothers and sisters in Christ?

God also promises us a rich future as children of God. In heaven, people of every race and from around the globe will gather. Heaven promises to be a place of great joy and celebration as we experience God's presence.

7. Look up the following passages. What does each one reveal about heaven and our future?

Revelation 7:16–17:

Revelation 14:13:

Revelation 21:4:

Revelation 21:7:

8. What aspect of being a child of God is the most meaningful to you—
calling on God as Father, receiving an eternal inheritance, becoming
part of the family of God, the promise of eternity with God, or another
aspect? Explain. Spend some time thanking God for the privilege of
being His child.

You are God's child!
As children of God, we have the
privilege of knowing God as our Father.
We are promised an eternal inheritance,
ushered into the family of God, and given
abundant promises regarding our
future in heaven with Him.

Digging Deeper

Read 1 Peter 1:13–16. As children of God, we're called to obey our
heavenly Father and walk in obedience to Him and His ways. In what
area of your life do you sense God calling you to greater obedience as
His child? What's preventing you from responding?

✤ Personal Challenge

Over the course of the next week, go online and use a website that allows you to search the Scripture, such as Biblegateway.com, to look up the word "Father" in the Gospels. Write down the passages that speak of God as Father and prayerfully consider how God wants to reveal Himself to you as your loving heavenly Father who wants to care for you in every way.

> "Just as He chose us in Him before the foundation of the world, that we should be holy and without blame before Him in love."

Ephesians 1:4

Handpicked by God

Several years ago, everything felt as though it were unraveling and nothing made sense. I prayed and cried out to God, yet all I heard was silence. I began wondering, "God, where are You? Do You even hear me at all?"

In the midst of this challenging season of life, my husband and I escaped on a much-needed getaway to a small mountain town. When we arrived, we discovered an outdoor festival was taking place in the downtown area. Small booths of companies promoting their goods lined the central city park. We strolled from vendor to vendor to see their offerings.

At one booth, we were invited to fill out a small raffle to win a pair of sporty sunglasses. The vendor explained they'd be giving out one pair of sunglasses on the hour every hour for the next three hours. To win, we needed to be present for the drawing. My husband and I dropped our tickets into the bin.

When we returned for the first drawing, we found a crowd gathered around the booth. Several tickets were drawn and those who won received smaller prizes—a water bottle, T-shirt, and sunscreen. Then the time came for the grand prize drawing of the sunglasses. I held our two tickets in my hand. The vendor hand picked a ticket and called out our number. We won!

After selecting a pair of sunglasses, the vendor explained that the winners' tickets would be returned to the bin for the next hourly drawing. When we returned an hour later for the grand prize of the sunglasses, we were astounded. Our ticket was hand-selected again! We stood in awe of the chances of winning twice in a row.

> Sometimes circumstances and situations in life cause us to begin wondering, "God, where are you?"

An hour later, we returned for the third and final drawing of the afternoon. As the vendor reached into the bin to hand-select the grand prize winner, he announced, "Surely it can't happen again." Then he read the numbers. We won a third and final time.

"I've never seen anything like this," he said. "It's like yours is the only ticket I can draw."

My husband and I looked at each other. We had already won two pairs of sunglasses and knew someone in the crowd could use the third pair of glasses more than we could. We asked the vendor to redraw so someone else could have a chance of winning.

Through this experience during a difficult season of life, I sensed God reminding me, *Margaret, you're going through a difficult time, but never doubt that I've got your number! Like those tickets, I've handpicked you, and I'm with you right in the midst of this.*

Sometimes circumstances and situations in life cause us to begin wondering, "God, where are You?" We may cry out in prayer with no response. We may assume God has bigger and better things to be taking care of or that He's no longer interested in our well-being.

But God knows our number. Nothing escapes God's notice. Not only has God hand-selected us, but He knows every detail of our lives. Even when God feels distant and unapproachable, passages such as Psalm 139 remind us that He handpicked and intimately created us. And He can do the impossible anytime He chooses in order to remind us of His presence and tender care.

1. When in your life have you been reminded that you were hand-selected by God, He knows your number, and no detail of your life has escaped His notice?

2. Do you tend to see everyday circumstances more as a result of happenstance or as divinely orchestrated by God? Mark your answer on the continuum below. Then explain your answer.

●━━━━━━━━━━━━━━━━━━━━━━━━━━━●

I tend to attribute things to happenstance.　　　　　　　　**I tend to attribute things to God.**

God handpicked you. He selected you. And He has a plan for your life that exceeds your wildest expectations.

3. Look up the following passages. What does each scripture reveal about God's purposes in hand-selecting you?

John 15:16:

2 Thessalonians 2:13–15:

1 Peter 2:9–10:

Since you are God's child, He knows you intimately. No detail of your life goes unnoticed by God.

4. **Read Psalm 139:1–6**. In the space below, write down everything God knows about you according to this passage. Which surprises you the most? Why?

5. What kinds of situations tempt you to believe the details of your life have escaped God's notice? How does this kind of thinking affect your outlook on life? Your relationship with God?

As you are hand-selected by God, He promises to never leave you. He is with you through the trials and triumphs of life.

6. **Read Psalm 139:7–12**. Do you tend to be more aware of God's presence in good times or troubled times? Explain.

God knows your strengths and weaknesses, your personality and quirks. He loves you just as you are!

7. **Read Psalm 139:13–16**. What encouragement do you find from realizing God knows so much about you?

God hand-selected you to grow into the fullness of all He has for you.

8. **Read Colossians 3:12–17**. In the chart below mark how difficult the quality from the passage is for you to embody: easy, medium, or hard. Circle the quality you most want God to develop in your life. Then ask Him to specifically develop this quality in you.

Quality	Easy	Medium	Hard
Mercy			
Kindness			
Humility			
Meekness			
Longsuffering			
Bearing with others			
Forgiving others			
Love			
Peace			
Thanksgiving			

Spend time in prayer asking God to fill you with the confidence and awareness of His presence. From the mundane to the crucial, He is at your side and loves you no matter what.

> You are hand-selected by God! God chose you before the foundation of the world to know Him and bring Him glory through your life. No detail escapes His notice.

Digging Deeper

Read Jeremiah 29:11. Thousands of years ago, God saved, led, healed, protected, and guided the Israelites out of Egyptian captivity and into the Promised Land. In the same way, God saves, leads, heals, protects, and guides us. Not only did He handpick us, just as He did the Israelites, but He has a plan and purpose for our lives too. When are you most tempted to doubt God has a plan and purpose in your life? When you look back on your life right now, where do you specifically see God unfolding the plan and purposes He has for you?

✤ Personal Challenge

Over the course of the next week, ask God to make you sensitive to His presence in your life. Each day, make a list of the specific ways you recognized God at work in your life. Share a handful of these with the group next time you meet.

"There is a friend *who* sticks closer than a brother."

Proverbs 18:24

Dear Friend of God

When Abram was the ripe age of seventy-five, God called him to leave behind everything familiar and journey to an unknown land. God promised to make Abram a great nation, bless him, make his name great, and bless others through him. Abram responded with obedience. He packed up his household, including his nephew Lot, and headed toward the Promised Land.

During a severe famine, Abram decided to make a detour and travel to Egypt. Unfortunately, he didn't bother to ask God's opinion and ended up in a pickle of a situation. He falsely claimed he wasn't married to his wife, Sarai. The next thing he knew, the pharaoh of Egypt was ready to take Sarai as his own wife—and he would have done it if God hadn't afflicted Pharaoh with a plague. When Pharaoh found out Abram's deception was the source of his affliction, he quickly sent Abram, Sarai, and everyone with them packing.

Despite the deception, God continued to bless Abram. Abram and Lot's livestock began multiplying to the extent that the land couldn't support them both. Abram generously gave Lot the pick of the pastures, and Lot chose the better land. Abram received the less lush land but responded by worshiping God as soon as he settled. Soon after, Lot discovered the grass wasn't really greener on his side of the pasture. Lot was taken prisoner by some bandits and Uncle Abram came to his rescue.

Again, God approached Abram to repeat the promise of land and renewed His commitment that Abram's descendants would be as numerous as the stars in the night sky. Yet Abram and his wife remained barren.

Frustrated by the lack of fruitfulness in their lives, they decided to take matters into their own hands. Sarai suggested that Hagar, their maid, become a surrogate mother. Abram agreed, and soon Ishmael was born. Despite the excitement of the arrival of a newborn, Sarai's heart grew cold toward Hagar and Ishmael, and the maid was forced to flee for her life.

Despite their impatience, God approached Abram again to inaugurate the promise that began thirteen years before (Genesis 15). Abram entered into a covenant signified by the rite of circumcision (owie!). Abram and his wife received new names: Abraham and Sarah. Soon after, some surprise visitors delivered striking news: when they returned the next year, Sarah would have a child. Overhearing the conversation, Sarah burst into laughter, thinking this promise impossible. The visitor asked if anything was impossible for God—a challenge to Sarah, Abraham, and us today.

The visitors' prophetic words came true. Sarah gave birth to Isaac, whose name means "laughter." At some point years later, God commanded Abraham to sacrifice Isaac in the land of Moriah as a sign of faithfulness. At the last moment, an angel of the Lord interrupted Abraham, and Isaac's

> The visitor asked if anything was impossible for God—a challenge to Sarah, Abraham, and us today.

life was spared. Abraham lived to be 175 years old—almost two centuries of walking with God.

Along the way, Abraham experienced the spectrum of highs and lows of journeying with God. At times, he fell prey to deception and lack of trust. Other times, he stood strong and chose faith and faithfulness in the face of adversity and trails. Along the way, Abraham demonstrated moments of radical obedience. Today, Abraham is heralded as the great patriarch, a father of faith.

But another title is also given to Abraham: friend of God.

This description of Abraham as God's friend appears multiple times throughout the Scripture, including Isaiah 41:8 and James 2:23. Through Abraham's story and faithfulness, we're reminded that each of us is invited to be not just a follower of God but a friend of God. We're invited to know God intimately and personally through the highs and lows of life—to know God like Abraham knew God. The Creator of the universe not only calls us "friend" but desires to walk in greater intimacy and affection with us each and every day. This is an invitation to friendship we don't want to miss.

1. What does being a friend of God mean to you?

2. When in your spiritual journey have you felt closest to God? Most far away?

3. What are some of the biggest challenges of being a friend of God?

Jesus rocks the world of His followers when He calls them friends. John 15 is part of Jesus' farewell discourse to His disciples before He was arrested, crucified, and resurrected from the grave. Jesus offered bold instructions of what following Him and bearing fruit for the Father's glory looks like. Ultimately, Jesus contrasted what being a servant of God—one who inherits nothing—and a friend of God—one who inherits love and salvation—means.

4. **Read John 15:13–15**. What is the difference between being a servant and a friend? In your life, do you tend to think of yourself as more of a servant or a friend of God? Explain.

Finding a close friend doesn't happen in a day. Friendships take time and effort to cultivate and strengthen. If you aren't spending time or energy on your friendships, they often fade. In the same way, God desires you to spend time and energy to strengthen your relationship with Him.

5. Which of the following spiritual disciplines are the most helpful in growing your friendship with God? Place a star by each one. What activities would you add to the list?

_____ Reading Scripture   _____ Spiritual retreats

_____ Praying   _____ Journaling

_____ Fasting   _____ Memorizing Scripture

_____ Silence   _____ Sharing your faith

Jesus does more than just *call* us His friends; through certain passages we see Him *living out* the practice of friendship when He walked the earth.

6. Read the following passages. What actions or descriptions demonstrate Jesus' friendships with His followers?

John 11:5:

John 11:28–35:

John 13:23:

John 21:1–9:

7. What three things are currently preventing you from developing a more vibrant, intimate friendship with God? (examples: busyness, distraction)

✣ _____

✣ _____

✣ _____

Sometimes, engaging in simple spiritual disciplines like reading the Bible, memorizing Scripture, and prayer can help us grow closer to God.

8. What three changes can you make in your life to nurture a more vibrant, intimate friendship with God?

✤ _____

✤ _____

✤ _____

Spend time asking God to draw you nearer into relationship and friendship with Him. Ask for a heart to pursue and cultivate the friendship over the next week.

Just like Abraham, we are invited to journey through the highs and lows of life with God by our side. God offers ultimate friendship and desires to grow in greater intimacy with us day by day.

Digging Deeper

Though Moses isn't directly called a friend of God as Abraham was, the Scripture refers to God speaking to Moses as a friend. **Read Exodus 33:7–23**. What does this passage reveal about the special relationship between Moses and God? What can you learn about the way you approach God from the way Moses approached God?

✤ Personal Challenge

Commit to spending at least ten minutes each day nurturing your friendship with God. Take time out of your schedule to sit quietly with God and talk to Him as you would a friend. Ask God to reveal to you how you can be a better friend and draw closer in your relationship with Him.

"To the praise of the glory of His grace, by
which He made us accepted in the Beloved."

Ephesians 1:6

Much Beloved of God

God loves you more than you know. Don't breeze by these
words, but pause, savor, and allow their truth to sink in. God refers
to you as part of the "the Beloved" (Ephesians 1:6). He loves you
with an everlasting love. He adores you.

One of the best descriptions of the love God has for you is
found in 1 Corinthians 13. Often when this passage is read, especially
at weddings, we think about its meaning in the way we love others.
But have you considered this is the way God loves you?

> [God's] love suffers long *and* is kind; [God's] love does not envy;
> [God's] love does not parade itself, [God's love] is not puffed
> up; [God's love] does not behave rudely, [God's love] does not
> seek its own, [God's love] is not provoked, [God's love] thinks
> no evil; [God's love] does not rejoice in iniquity, but rejoices in
> the truth; [God's love] bears all things, [God's love] believes all
> things, [God's love] hopes all things, [God's love] endures all
> things. [God's] love never fails. (1 Corinthians 13:4–8, *"God's
> love" added for emphasis*)

And nothing can separate you from this love!

In the book of Romans, Paul wrote, "For I am persuaded that neither death nor life, nor angels nor principalities nor powers, nor things present nor things to come, nor height nor depth, nor any other created thing, shall be able to separate us from the love of God which is in Christ Jesus our Lord" (Romans 8:38–39).

Consider that absolutely nothing, nada, zip, zero can separate us from God's love.

This means the hardest things we face in life can't pry the love of God away from us.

✤ Raising children can't separate us from the love of God.

✤ Wrestling with an addiction can't separate us from the love God.

✤ Facing life's toughest trials can't separate us from the love of God.

✤ Marital difficulties can't separate us from the love of God.

✤ Being fired can't separate us from the love of God.

✤ Going bankrupt can't separate us from the love of God.

✤ Changes in lifestyle can't separate us from the love of God.

✤ Retirement can't separate us from the love of God.

✤ Loneliness can't separate us from the love of God.

✤ Burying a loved one can't separate us from the love of God.

✤ Facing a chronic or terminal illness can't separate us from the love God.

In everything, the love of God remains. The love God has for you now will remain for all of eternity. Though we may face challenges and difficulties that cause us to doubt or second-guess God's love, He remains relentless in His affection for us. All you need to do is receive it. Indeed, you are much beloved of God!

1. When was the last time someone told you he or she loved you and you felt his or her love vibrant in your heart? How did you feel afterward? How did those words change your outlook on life and the way you saw others?

2. How do you tend to think about God's love? Mark your response on the continuum below.

●━━━━━━━━━━━━━━━━━━━━━━●

**I tend to think of
God loving other
people.**

**I tend to think of
God personally
loving me.**

3. What prevents you from experiencing more of God's love in your life?

4. In the space below, write out Isaiah 43:1. Replace "O Jacob" and "O Israel" with your name. How does personalizing this Scripture affect the way you read it?

5. What do the following passages reveal about God's love for you? Which of these is most meaningful in your life? Why?

Psalm 108:4:

Joel 2:13:

Isaiah 54:10:

Romans 8:32:

The love God has for you is meant to flow through you to others. God wants to fill you up with so much of His love that it literally splashes out of your life. At times, you won't even be aware this is happening.

6. **Read Ephesians 5:2**. Who is our standard for loving others? In the past week, when have you specifically struggled to show love to someone? How did you handle the situation?

Romans 12 is often called the "Little Bible" because of its quick overview of Christ's message. Often in Paul's writings, a shift occurs between the doctrinal section and the practical application. In Romans, chapters 1–11 are doctrinal and 12–15 are practical. Paul described how to practically live out faith in Christ.

7. **Read Romans 12:9–21**. According to this passage, what are the attitudes, responses, and behaviors of someone walking in Christ's love?

8. Which are the three most difficult attitudes, responses, and behaviors for you to practice right now?

Spend some time prayerfully asking God to infuse you with His love so you may show it to others in every situation you face.

God's love is unconditional and endless. He relentlessly and passionately loves you—His beloved.

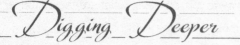

Digging Deeper

Read 1 John 3:18. What does loving in word mean for you? Loving in tongue? Deed? Truth? With which of those is it easiest for you to love people? Which is most challenging? Why? Spend some time asking God to give you grace to love people in all these ways. Look for opportunities God may present in the upcoming week.

✤ Personal Challenge

On a blank piece of paper, create a list of ten ways God has demonstrated His love to you this week. Then spend time thanking God for creating and lavishing you with His love.

> "For You have made him most blessed forever;
> You have made him exceedingly glad with
> Your presence."

Psalm 21:6

Abundantly Blessed by God

When was the last time you counted your blessings? How high did the number reach? Does the list of blessings in your life really have an end? As children of God, we're blessed beyond our wildest imaginations.

While some of the lessons in this study begin by sharing a story of what God has done in someone else's life, this lesson is about recognizing the good things God has done in your life. You're invited to write down the many ways God has shown Himself to be generous, faithful, and kind to you. To help you count the blessings of God in your life, fill out the chart below. Use each letter of the alphabet, from A to Z, to write down a word or phrase describing a moment in your life or a specific experience revealing one of God's blessings in your life. You may want to write a person's name, a moment of provision, a meaningful gift, or an instance of divine strength or grace in which God revealed His love for you.

A age
B breakfast Bible
C cars
D daughters (great)
E ears
F family
G gcand girls
H house
I ice cream
J Jaws
K kitchen
L life
M money
N meats
O oatmeal
P peanuts popcorn
Q quiet time Quander
R rest Randy
S schools
T teachers
U uncles
V values veggies

W _*water*_

X _*x rays*_

Y _*Yogurt.*_

Z _*zoos*_

When writing to the church of Ephesus, the apostle Paul declared, "Blessed *be* the God and Father of our Lord Jesus Christ, who has blessed us with every spiritual blessing in the heavenly *places* in Christ" (Ephesians 1:3). That's a powerful reminder that we can praise God for both the seen and unseen blessings in our lives.

When we take a few moments to remember God's blessings, we become all the more grateful to be God's children. His blessings anchor us in the unending goodness and love of God and draw us even more into His embrace.

1. What did the list you made of God's blessings in your life reveal about God's love and care for you?

2. Which of the blessings you listed were most surprising or long forgotten? Explain.

3. What are three benefits of remembering and recognizing the blessings of God in your life?

You are abundantly blessed in Christ, and all these blessings mean you are to be a blessing to others—in your family, your neighborhood, your workplace, and your community.

Abraham was abundantly blessed by God, and God reminded him of his opportunity to bless others. Genesis 12:1–3 describes God's encounter with Abraham, when a covenant was established—a promise of blessing to Abraham and his lineage. God also established covenants through Noah (Genesis 9:1–17), Moses (the 613 commandments in the Torah), David (2 Samuel 7:12–13), and ultimately, Christ (Hebrews 9:15).

4. **Read Genesis 12:1–3**. What did God promise to bless Abraham with in this passage? What was the purpose of God's blessing for Abraham (hint: verse 3)?

5. Do you tend to think of God's blessing as something given to you or something meant to flow through you?

After being oppressed in Egypt for more than four hundred years, the Israelites followed Moses out of slavery and into the wilderness. God miraculously provided water, bread, and meat for His people during their journey into the Promised Land.

Rather than give the Israelites a buffet-style smorgasbord, God put regulations on His blessings—not to burden but to remind each person to place their trust in God each day.

6. **Read Exodus 16:10–20**. How did Moses' instruction regarding the manna challenge the Israelites to depend on God?

On the sixth day, the Israelites gathered two portions of manna. On the seventh day, the Israelites refrained from gathering manna. This was not just a day of rest for the Israelites, but God entered into rest with the Israelites as He withheld from providing food on the seventh day.

7. When have you stored up the blessings of God and found them rotting later?

8. What abundant blessing has God provided you with that you sense He is nudging you to share with others? What's holding you back?

Spend time in prayer asking God to fill your heart with a desire to acknowledge and share the gifts He offers. Anchor yourself in the unending goodness and love of God and draw even closer to His embrace.

God longs to bless you and abundantly bless others through you.

Digging Deeper

Throughout the Bible, God reminds us He wants to bless those who follow His commands and walk in righteousness. But there are also ramifications of making poor decisions and rebelling against God. **Read Deuteronomy 11:26–30**. When have you experienced the blessing that comes with obeying God and following His commands? When have you experienced the curse, loss, or pain of choosing not to obey God? In what areas of your life do you need to choose to obey God in order to experience His provision, protection, and blessing?

✤ Personal Challenge

Taking the A-through-Z list from above, rewrite each blessing on a separate note card or Post-it note. Scatter them throughout your house, office, and car. Each time you see one of the twenty-six blessings, spend time thanking God for His hand in your life. For a greater challenge, create an attitude of gratitude notebook. Each day for a month, write down one thing, person, or event you are grateful for. Consider extending it throughout the year.

Transformed by God Again and Again

God performs
ongoing
transformational
work in the lives of all
His children. As people
wholly embraced by God,
we can celebrate His awesome
faithfulness and goodness taking
place each and every day in our
lives.

"Therefore, if anyone *is* in Christ, *he is* a
new creation; old things have passed away;
behold, all things have become new."

2 Corinthians 5:17

You Are New, New, New

A nurse in Australia spent several years working alongside
patients who were in the final three months of their lives. As she
worked, she kept track of the various insights and observations
of those for whom she cared. As she listened to each patient's
assessment of his or her life, she noticed that people at the end
of life tend to have a sense of clarity and wisdom worth learning
from.[1]

The nurse recorded the top five regrets of those facing
death. The first regret was that many patients wished they'd had
the courage to live more true to themselves instead of living the
life others expected them to live. Living to fulfill other people's
expectations meant many of their own goals and dreams remained
unfulfilled.

Another common regret patients had was wishing they hadn't
worked so hard. Putting in the extra hours meant they missed
some of their children's sporting events and activities. At times,

their marriages suffered. And they didn't take enough time to enjoy the gift of life.

Those facing the end of life also wished they'd had the courage to express their feelings. Many noted they had suppressed how they really felt in an effort to appease others. Some even developed illnesses as a result of the resentment they carried.

Patients also wished they had stayed in touch with friends. Through the busyness of life, many let friendships wane and lost track of personal relationships. With the days of their lives counting down, many wanted to track down friends, but some proved hard to find. The nurse noted everyone missed his or her friends when he or she was dying.

And the fifth, biggest regret the patients had was that they had not allowed themselves to be happier. Many patients did not realize until the end that happiness is a choice. Rather than make the choice, some patients clung to what was familiar—old patterns and habits rather than making decisions that would bring them greater contentment and joy.

Such discoveries provide wisdom for those who want to make the most of their lives. The good news is, as a child of God, you don't have to live or die with regret. With God, nothing is beyond healing, redemption, transformation, or change—including you! Through the grace and strength of God, you can make changes and decisions that will leave you without regret.

God called you a "new creation," and the work God is doing in your life is always new, new, new (2 Corinthians 5:17). You are being transformed by God each day to become more like Christ—and this is not only good but exciting news. With God, every day is a new beginning.

> The good news is, as children of God, you don't have to live or die with regret.

1. Reflecting on the patients' regrets from the introduction, which regret do you think you're most prone to having?

2. What is your greatest regret in life so far? What are you doing to make changes in your life to not live with any regrets?

God has been making things new since creation. The book of Isaiah is prophetic literature composed by multiple authors over a span of two centuries. As a whole, the book of Isaiah prophesies about the work God was doing in the lives of His people—the Israelites—before, during, and after their Babylonian captivity.

3. **Read Isaiah 43:18–19**. What hope do you find in this particular passage about the work God is doing in your life?

4. **Read Isaiah 42:5–9**. When in the last year have you sensed God doing a new work in your life?

Through a new job, new city, new school, new friend, or newfound hope or confidence, God is always making things new in and around us.

Lamentations reminds us of the new work God did in the lives of the Israelites while they were in captivity by the Babylonians. In chapters one and two, the unknown author of Lamentations wrote of the struggles they endured—including the destruction of the temple in Jerusalem. Starting in Lamentations 3:22, the author remembered God's faithfulness.

5. **Read Lamentations 3:19–26**. What shift in perspective did the author have within this passage? When in the last year have you sensed God doing a new work in the life of someone you know and love?

Throughout Scripture—from Genesis to Revelation—the theme of the potter and clay is expressed and amplified. Reminding us of God's sovereignty, this symbol is expressed to display God's intimate involvement in our lives.

6. **Read Isaiah 45:9–10**. What does the imagery of a potter and clay suggest to you about the way God is working in your life?

God brings newness in relationships, jobs, communities, church families, friends, and neighbors. Sometimes the new work God accomplishes is on the inside—offering peace, affirmation, confidence, and hope.

7. **Read Revelation 21:5**. In what area of your life do you currently sense God reshaping you? What are you learning about God through the process?

8. In what area of your life do you most want God to do a new work?

Spend some time prayerfully asking God to begin reshaping and renewing you.

With God, nothing is beyond His healing, redemption, transformation, or change—including you! You can live without regret.

Digging Deeper

Jesus healed countless men and women during His earthly ministry. With each encounter, people's lives were transformed forever. **Read Matthew 8:1–17**. Make a list of all the people Jesus began a new work in. How do you think each person's life was transformed? Spend some time asking God to bring healing and transformation into your life.

✤ Personal Challenge

On a blank sheet of paper, make a list of the regrets you fear you'll have at the end of your life. Spend time prayerfully asking God about what changes or decisions you need to make in your life so you can live without regret and walk in the fullness of all God has for you.

"For we are His workmanship, created in Christ Jesus for good works, which God prepared beforehand that we should walk in them."

Ephesians 2:10

You Are God's Masterpiece

If you've visited the Black Hills of South Dakota, then you've probably seen the President's Mountain, also known as Mount Rushmore. Four presidents are carved into the mountain—George Washington, Thomas Jefferson, Theodore Roosevelt, and Abraham Lincoln.

The idea for the project was developed by Doane Robinson. He wanted to create an attraction to draw people from around the nation to visit South Dakota. He began working with President Calvin Coolidge and congress to win support for the project. Congress agreed to match up to $250,000 of funding, and Gutzon Borglum was hired as the sculptor. Borglum and a team of four hundred workers sculpted the masterpiece. The project took fourteen years to complete and was dedicated on October 31, 1941.

Today, the faces of the four presidents stand fifty-five hundred feet above sea level. Each head is as tall as a six-story building.

The colossal memorial is breathtaking, and nearly three million people from around the world visit annually.

But a look in history books or a quick search online of the area before October 4, 1927, reveals a very different portrait of Mount Rushmore—images of the mountain before the carving made it famous. Old black-and-white photos show a rugged mountain laced with ponderosa. A quick comparison of the before and after photos of Mount Rushmore is profound, providing a glimpse into the ongoing work God is doing in our lives.

God is patient, diligent, and wholly committed to His work.

As we continue to seek God, we find that He, like a master sculptor, carves away our hardened exteriors to reveal the image of God residing within each of us. God is patient, diligent, and wholly committed to His work. He patiently chips away at false beliefs that stand in the way of our relationship with Him, and continues to reveal the truth of who He is and all He's created us to be. No matter where you are in life, you are God's masterpiece and you can rest assured God isn't done with you yet. And He has a vision for your future that's better than anything you can imagine.

1. What is a craft, project, or event you've taken (or seen someone else take) from start to finish? How is this transformation reflected in your life or the lives of those around you?

The apostle Paul (whose story will be shared later in this chapter) wrote the book of Ephesians while imprisoned in Rome. Paul addressed many issues in the church of Ephesus, such as fragments and divisions within the body of believers—much like those that exist in many churches today.

2. **Read Ephesians 2:10**. Write the verse in the space below and underline any words or phrases that are particularly meaningful to you.

The word "workmanship" comes from the Greek word *poiema*, meaning "poem." The term suggests God is the Author of our lives creating works of beauty within us. The only other place in the New Testament where this word occurs is Romans 1:20.

3. **Read Romans 1:20**. The phrase "the things that are made" refers to God's workmanship. According to this passage, where is God's workmanship or "poem" found? In what ways are you experiencing God the Poet writing His story in you right now?

It was not by coincidence that the apostle Paul used the idea of God's workmanship, especially considering all the transformation he had experienced in his life. At first glance, Saul (later known as Paul) was an unlikely choice for an apostle. Before he had a profound encounter with God, he was famous for persecuting Christians.

4. **Read Acts 7:54—8:3**. How does the Bible portray Saul's attitude and outlook on life and faith?

At the time, Jews taught their children a specific trade to live by in addition to what they learned attending school. Saul studied Jewish law under renowned Pharisee Gamaliel and was a tent-stitcher by family trade. Despite Saul's zealous beliefs that made him hate Christ-followers, God created something new and beautiful in and through his life.

5. **Read Acts 9:1–19**. What transformed Saul? Describe a time when you went through a difficult situation and recognized God more clearly afterward. How did the experience transform you?

The transformation in Saul's life made him almost unrecognizable to others.

6. **Read Acts 9:20–31**. What were some specific outward signs of Saul's transformation? What are some specific outward signs in your life from moments when God transformed you?

While he might have considered himself unredeemable and unusable by God, Saul's transformation led to the good news of Jesus spreading all over what is now modern-day Greece and Turkey.

7. **Read 1 Timothy 1:15–17.** How did Paul (formerly named Saul) describe the transformation that happened in his life? How had Paul become God's masterpiece?

8. In what three areas of your life do you most want to experience God's transformative power and work right now?

Spend some time asking God to continue the work He's doing in and through you to become His masterpiece.

You are God's masterpiece—and He is working in and through you in ways more spectacular than you can imagine.

Digging Deeper

Read Philippians 1:3–6. Why do you think God is so committed to completing the work He has begun in you? What does such a commitment reveal about God? About you? When are you most likely to doubt this promise in your life? When are you most likely to believe it?

✤ Personal Challenge

Pull out a blank sheet of paper and create a list of all the ways God has been transforming you. Think about how God has been changing your perspective, outlook, and attitude toward Him and others, as well as the growing fruit of the Spirit in your life (Galatians 5:22–23). Take time to thank God for the work He is doing.

> "Therefore we also, since we are surrounded
> by so great a cloud of witnesses, let us
> lay aside every weight, and the sin which
> so easily ensnares *us*, and let us run with
> endurance the race that is set before us."

Hebrews 12:1

You Are Part of God's Big Family

Four hundred meters stood between Derek Redmond and the medal stand at the 1992 Barcelona Olympics. Though he was favored to win gold, the road to this Olympic race had been tough for Redmond. The British sprinter had broken records and won world championships, but this was his first opportunity to run an Olympic race. Injuries had prevented him from racing in previous Olympics.

As the athletes planted their feet in place, Jim Redmond, Derek's father, cheered in anticipation from the top row of the sixty-five-thousand-person stadium.

The starting gun fired. Runners exploded off the starting line. Derek stole the early lead. Then unexpectedly, with only 175 meters to go, Derek's right hamstring shredded. He collapsed on the track in agonizing pain. Competitors whizzed by as Derek watched his Olympic dream crumble.

Paramedics soon arrived with a stretcher to assist Derek off the track. He waved them away. Determined to finish, he stood up and began hobbling toward the finish line. The crowd roared.

Meanwhile, the moment Jim Redmond watched his son fall, he stood up and began elbowing his way to the sideline. Without credentials, he leaped over the gate, pushed past security guards, and ran to Derek. Nothing was going to come between this dad and his son.

Jim wrapped his arms around his son, tears streaming down his face, and carried him toward the finish line. He said, "I am here, son; we'll finish this together."[1]

> "I am here, son. we'll finish this together."

The two staggered together for the final 120 meters cheered on by tens of thousands of fans who leaped to their feet in a standing ovation. Right before the finish line, Jim released Derek so he could cross the finish line on his own. Throwing his arms around him once again, Jim announced he was the proudest father alive—prouder than if his son had won the gold medal.

In an interview after the event, Jim told the camera he was there at the beginning of Derek's career, so he might as well be there at the end. Becoming an Olympic athlete isn't a one-person job. Derek's coaches, trainers, friends, and family encouraged and challenged him over the years. And his dad continued to support him—even to the end.

In the book of Philippians, the apostle Paul described the Christian life as a race—one we endure and press on toward the goal. But like Derek Redmond, it's not a journey we make on our own, but one where people surround us and encourage us along the way.

We can't become all God has created us to be on our own. We need each other. God knows this and He's designed us to live in relationship with others. We are part of God's big family—the body of Christ. Through our brothers and sisters in Christ, we can press on through the race marked out for us and play our role in God's restoration of the world.

1. Just like Jim Redmond came alongside his son in his time of need, who has come alongside of you during trying times?

2. Who have you come alongside to support and cheer on in life and faith? How did serving and encouraging someone else affect your faith?

Each of God's children is created with different gifts and talents. When we offer those gifts alongside others in the body of Christ, we become part of God's larger purpose for the world.

In 1 Corinthians 12:12–31, the apostle Paul addressed two audiences who had very different understandings of what being part of God's family meant. The first audience (verses 14–20) was made up of those who felt their role and gifting in the body of Christ were unimportant. Like the appendix in a human body, these people didn't feel as though they had a purpose.

The second group of people Paul addressed (verses 21–31) had the opposite problem. They felt overly confident and arrogant about their roles and talents. They labeled parts of the body as less essential or valuable than others.

3. **Read 1 Corinthians 12:14–20.** Describe a time in your life when you felt unimportant and needed to be encouraged. Who was a source of encouragement during that time in your life? What encouragement do you find from this passage?

4. Describe a time in your life when you felt as though your role or your gifts were crucial to a situation and you fell prey to becoming arrogant or overconfident. What did you learn through the situation? What encouragement do you find from 1 Corinthians 12:21–26?

God created each of us with unique gifts to be shared. We have the opportunity to serve others by using these God-given gifts— whether teaching, singing, encouraging, giving, or serving—to the glory of God. We play our part in God's family when we use the gifts we've been entrusted with to the fullest extent possible.

5. **Read Romans 12:3–8.** What specific gifts do you think God has given you to be used to bring Him glory? How are you being intentional about using your gifts right now? Are there any gifts you feel like you're burying or not using to their full extent? Explain.

As we worship, work, and play alongside others in God's family, we can take every opportunity to cheer each other along in the journey of faith.

Throughout Paul's writings, we read about his friend Barnabas and his mentee Timothy—a younger pastor. When we have people like Paul, Barnabas, and Timothy in our lives, we can't help but grow in our relationship with God. A "Paul" is a wise mentor who leads the way. A "Barnabas" is the person running alongside experiencing the same things. "Timothy" is someone you can pour into and lead.

6. In the space below, consider the roles of Paul, Barnabas, and Timothy and who is currently filling them in your life.

✤ My Paul:

✤ My Barnabas:

✤ My Timothy:

7. Not only are we challenged to find our Paul, Barnabas, and Timothy, but we need to be Paul, Barnabas, and Timothy to others. In the space below, consider who you're encouraging, growing alongside, and learning from.

✤ I am Paul to:

✤ I am Barnabas to:

✤ I am Timothy to:

8. Who are three fellow believers in your life you can show the love of Christ to this week? Write their names below and commit to being a voice of encouragement in their lives.

✤ _____

✤ _____

✤ _____

Spend time in prayer asking God to provide opportunities and willingness to live out your gifts.

Through our relationships with others who are God's children, we will grow into all God has created us to be.

Digging Deeper

Through Jesus, we are all welcomed with outstretched arms into God's big family. **Read Ephesians 2:19–22**. What does being part of God's household mean? How does this look different from being a stranger or foreigner to God's household? What changes do you need to make in your life right now to become better connected to the family of God?

✤ Personal Challenge

Take a spiritual gifts test to find out the specific gifts and talents God has equipped you with. Use a resource like the Clifton StrengthsFinder, found at www.strengthstest.com, or search for "spiritual gifts test" online. Spend time in prayer asking God to put you in situations where you will be able to recognize and use your gifts.

Bonus Activity

Visit YouTube and search for "Perseverance Derek Redmond." Take a few minutes to watch the footage of Derek Redmond's race. Spend time in prayer asking God to show you whose life He's asking you to become involved in and cheer someone on.

"And the LORD, He *is* the One who goes before you. He will be with you, He will not leave you nor forsake you; do not fear nor be dismayed."

Deuteronomy 31:8

You Are Connected

Tucked deep into the Old Testament is a little book known as Ezra. Now Ezra is an old-time prophet we don't hear about often enough. He was a highly respected Jewish scribe and priest who came from the line of Moses' brother Aaron (Ezra 7:1–5). This small book of the Bible provides rich insights into our connection with God.

Many years ago, the nation of Israel was torn away from their sacred homeland. For seventy years they lived in exile in a place called Babylon; this time was often referred to as the Babylonian captivity. Despite being many miles from home and their temples, the Jewish people still maintained allegiance to God.

When they finally returned to their homeland, they had become different people. Not only did they speak a new language—adapting their Hebrew language into the Aramaic language—but they also kept track of time differently, making changes to their annual calendar. Their religious practices were impacted too. The

Torah—the first five books of the Old Testament—became central in their lives. But one of the most surprising changes that happened while they lived in captivity is that their view of God expanded.

Before they were dragged away from their homeland, the Jewish people were convinced God was fixed in one place. In essence, God was immobile. They believed God sat on a throne of the temple mount. The only way to approach God was to climb the mountain. In order to encounter God, you had to make a long ascension. Living in exile helped the Israelites realize God isn't tied to a particular latitude and longitude. God isn't static. God's presence knows no boundaries. He fills the earth. The Israelites learned that God remained with them—even in a foreign land—continuing to guide them, lead them, and shepherd them no matter where they went.

God's presence knows no boundaries.

This was a powerful discovery for the ancient Israelites, and it is a powerful discovery for each of us as we journey with God. Sometimes we may be tempted to believe God is in only one place—a particular building or church service or community. But God is everywhere, and He has designed you for relationship with Him. As God's child, you have full access to God anytime and anyplace. You are connected to Him.

1. When in your life do you tend to feel closest to God?

2. When in your life do you tend to feel as though you're the farthest away from God?

The idea of being connected to God appears throughout the Scripture. In the very beginning of Genesis, we receive a glimpse of what communicating with God in a perfect relationship looked like.

3. **Read Genesis 2:15–25**. What do you think was the best part about living in the garden of Eden? What do you imagine were some of the things Adam and Eve talked about with God before the forbidden fruit was eaten?

Yet even after their willful act of disobedience—eating from the off-limits tree—God did not go silent on humankind. He kept speaking to them, leading them, and guiding them.

4. **Read Genesis 3:8–23**. Where do you see the loving-kindness of God displayed in this passage? Where do you see God still clearly desired a relationship with humankind?

Even after the Fall, God continued passionately pursuing humankind. Outside of the borders of the garden, God continued revealing His love, faithfulness, and desire to be connected through relationship.

Through Jesus Christ, we have direct access to God around the clock. We are called into a greater level of connection with Christ where He remains faithful to the work He has begun with us.

5. **Read 1 Corinthians 1:9**. According to this passage, to what has God called you? How are you answering this call right now?

Not only does God call us into greater connection with Christ, we are called to abide in Christ's love so we can bear the fruit of the Spirit to the world. In John 15, John offered a parable (one of two in his gospel) comparing our spiritual lives with a vine.

6. **Read John 15:1–8**. What does abiding in Christ in the midst of your everyday look like?

7. When are you most aware you're not abiding in Christ? When are you most aware you are abiding in Christ?

We can stay connected to God through prayer, by spending time with other followers of Jesus, and also through studying the Scripture. The Bible is God's megaphone to His people. Often the words of Scripture will speak directly into situations and relationships in the midst of our everyday.

8. **Read Hebrews 4:12**. In the space below, draw a picture of what this verse is describing. How have you experienced this passage as true in your life? What changes do you need to make in order to nurture a greater sense of connection between you and God?

Spend time in prayer asking God for the desire and courage to cut back on "me time" and focus on "God time." Ask Him to infiltrate everything you do—from the mundane daily tasks to the big decisions—as you seek His wisdom and guidance each day.

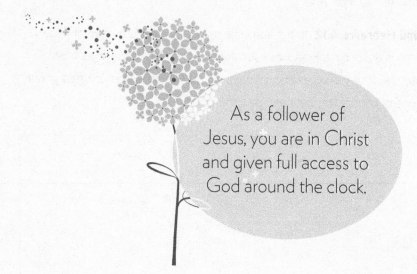

As a follower of Jesus, you are in Christ and given full access to God around the clock.

Digging Deeper

Ezra and Nehemiah recorded the fulfillment of God's promise to the Israelites as they returned to their land and rebuilt the temple after spending seventy years in Babylonian captivity. **Read Ezra 3:10–13.** How did different people respond to the temple's foundation being laid? Why do you think they responded in this way? How have you seen the way you connect to God grow and change over the years?

✤ Personal Challenge

This week commit Deuteronomy 31:8 to memory.
Write the passage on a few note cards and keep
them around the house or at work where you'll
naturally be reminded of this incredible promise.

"For I am persuaded that neither death nor
life, nor angels nor principalities nor powers,
nor things present nor things to come, nor
height nor depth, nor any other created
thing, shall be able to separate us from the
love of God which is in Christ Jesus our Lord."

Romans 8:38–39

You Are an Overcomer

Some would say the odds were against Dillon Coleman from
the beginning. While Dillon was still in his mother's womb, doctors
began noticing something wasn't developing properly in Dillon's
body: bones weren't growing in one of his hands.

Dillon arrived in this world without a left hand. Yet Dillon
refused to allow what was missing to hold him back. Like many
kids, he loved baseball. But all too often he found himself cut
from teams. Dillon refused to give up. He continued pursuing
his passion, and despite all odds he became a starter at Gordon
College in Massachusetts.

For Dillon, hitting a ball involves holding a 32-inch, 29-ounce
bat with one hand. He rests the bat on the bone of his left hand
and uses torque to lift the bat in every swing—not an easy task.
He refuses to talk about the disadvantage of trying to hit a baseball

or switch from glove to bare hand quick enough to throw someone out. Instead, he focuses on showing others what it means to use all the God-given gifts with which they've been entrusted.[1]

Dillon's is a powerful story of overcoming the odds. Though Dillon might have been tempted to focus on what he didn't have, he chose to invest his time and energy developing what he was given. He focused more on what was possible than what was impossible and became a mighty source of inspiration to others.

If we take a close look at our lives, we'll soon discover we all have areas that didn't develop fully. Even though our bodies may be whole and healthy, we may have other areas—in our background, relationships, communication, education, abilities, or emotions—where, like Dillon, we need to be overcomers. We have to make a choice: Will we focus on what we don't have or will we turn to God knowing nothing is impossible for Him? The Bible reminds us that through Christ every weakness and temptation can be overcome. Indeed, you are an overcomer.

If we take a close look at our lives, we'll soon discover we all have areas that didn't develop fully.

1. What is one area of your life you've had to overcome the odds to succeed? What role did God play in giving you the strength and grace to overcome?

As a child of God, you don't have to face the challenges of life or faith alone. God is with you! And God wants to equip you for every situation you'll face. In the book of Ephesians, the apostle Paul tells us our strength to overcome is found in God and His awesome power.

2. **Read Ephesians 6:10–18**. In the chart below fill out what each piece of armor represents.

Piece of Armor	Purpose
Belt	
Breastplate	
Foot Armor	
Shield	
Helmet	
Sword	

3. Which piece of armor are you most comfortable in wearing? Which piece of armor do you need to remember to put on each day?

In the book of Philippians, the apostle Paul challenged us to gird ourselves in a different kind of armor. He didn't use military images, but showed we could be overcomers as we take on the attitudes and perspectives of Christ.

4. **Read Philippians 4:4–13**. Make a list of all the things Paul advised in this passage knowing he could do anything through God's strength.

5. How does practicing these things in your life give you the strength to overcome difficult situations and circumstances? What happens when you don't practice these things?

The final book of the Bible, Revelation, highlights two keys to overcoming. John recorded that a loud voice from heaven will declare the victory in the final battle against the evil one.

6. **Read Revelation 12:11**. In what two ways did these saints triumph over the power of the enemy?

7. In three short sentences, write your personal testimony or story of what God has done in your life. How does sharing your story and listening to others' stories affect your faith?

At the end of Romans 8, Paul provided a powerful closing to his defense of the gospel. He closed with the reminder that if God is for us, who could be against us? Through God's love and Christ's work on the cross, we can overcome all condemnation, every temptation, even death.

8. **Read Romans 8:31–37.** How has God's love made you more than a conqueror? Make a list of three specific ways in which God's love has given you the strength, power, and grace to be an overcomer.

✤ _____

✤ _____

✤ _____

Spend some time praying about who you can show God's love to in order to help them overcome as well.

> With God, you can overcome anything. You are more than a conqueror through Jesus Christ.

Digging Deeper

Second Corinthians 4 is another instance where we see the symbolism of the clay and the potter, reminding us of the plans God has for us to display His glory. **Read 2 Corinthians 4**. How does Paul's attitude toward hardship compare to your own? How does your perspective and attitude change when you focus on the invisible and eternal?

✦ Personal Challenge

Use a search engine to find 2 Corinthians 4 online, then print out the entire chapter. Decorate the printout with a design and place it somewhere in your house where you can read and reflect on it regularly.

"But as many as received Him, to them He gave the right to become children of God, to those who believe in His name: who were born, not of blood, nor of the will of the flesh, nor of the will of man, but of God."

John 1:12–13

You Are Wholly God's Own

Remember where we began in this study. We looked at the idea that each of us wakes up with one big question every day. Whether or not we say it aloud to ourselves or someone else, a question lurks beneath the surface in our lives. Questions such as: Am I really loved? Why am I here? Does what I do matter? Do I matter? Do I really belong?

Throughout these lessons, we've been seeing what God has to say on those matters. We've been exploring the idea that you are God's wondrous child whom He's handpicked. You are not just invited to become a follower of Christ but are also a friend of the God who abounds in love and blessings. Because of this love, God is doing a transformative work in you, renewing and creating you to be His masterpiece. Whether you think of God's work in your life as that of a master sculptor or the finest poet, God is committed to the work He's begun in you. He's wired you for relationship with others and Himself. And with God, nothing is impossible. You are an overcomer.

Yet sometimes in the midst of our everyday, we can forget we're wholly embraced by God. This is why anchoring ourselves in the truths of what Scripture says about us is important. Through the following passages, consider what it means to be God's own and to find the fullness of our identities in Him.

✤ We are the light of the world.—Matthew 5:14

✤ We are God's children.—John 1:12

✤ We are justified by God.—Romans 5:1

✤ We are free from condemnation.—Romans 8:1–2

✤ We are united with Christ.—1 Corinthians 6:17

✤ We are not our own.—1 Corinthians 6:19

✤ We belong to God.—1 Corinthians 6:19

✤ We have been bought with a price.—1 Corinthians 6:20

✤ We are part of God's family.—1 Corinthians 12:27

✤ We are established by God.—2 Corinthians 1:21

✤ We are anointed by God.—2 Corinthians 1:21

✤ We are sealed by God.—2 Corinthians 1:22

✤ We are ambassadors for Christ.—2 Corinthians 5:20

✤ We are chosen by God.—Ephesians 1:3–8

✤ We are made holy by God.—Ephesians 1:4

✤ We are dearly loved by God.—Ephesians 2:4

✣ We are alive with Christ.—Ephesians 2:5

✣ We are rescued by God.—Colossians 1:13

✣ We are forgiven by God.—Colossians 1:14

✣ We are redeemed by God.—Colossians 1:14

✣ We have full access to God.—Hebrews 4:14–16

✣ We are protected by God.—1 John 5:18

God reminds us repeatedly that we are His workmanship, created to be loved, forgiven, protected, and so much more. As we read these promises and see ourselves through God's eyes, we can't help but turn back in thanksgiving to God.

No matter who we are or where we've been, God gently ushers us into His arms and whispers to us that we are His children. To think about the work God is doing in our lives when we commit ourselves to Him and become wholly His own is amazing!

1. Read aloud the scriptures from the list at the start of this lesson. Reflecting on these passages, which three are you most thankful for right now?

✣ _____

✣ _____

✣ _____

2. Reflecting on these passages, which three are you experiencing to be true in a new or fresh way in your own life right now? Explain.

❖ _____

❖ _____

❖ _____

3. Which of these passages do you most struggle to remember in the midst of your day-to-day?

4. What do you tend to think is God's attitude toward you? Angry? Disappointed? Celebratory? Joyful? Why do you tend to think that? What do the verses in the introduction reveal about God's attitude toward you?

5. The Bible reveals what God thinks about you. Who of the following tends to influence what you think about yourself the most?

_____ Mom or Dad   _____ Teachers

_____ Family   _____ Boss

_____ Co-workers   _____ Media

_____ Community   _____ Popular culture

_____ Neighbors   _____ Spiritual leader/Mentor

_____ Scripture

6. How do you think reading or reflecting on these passages on a regular basis will affect your outlook on life? On God? Others?

7. Reflect on the opening idea of this study that we all have one question we ask ourselves. Has God provided you an answer through this study? If so, what specific scripture has He answered your big question with?

8. What is one practical step you can take this week to remember your identity as God's beloved child to whom He is wholly committed?

Spend time in prayer thanking God you are His beloved child. Ask God to penetrate your heart with how cherished you are by Him and to divinely place you in conversations where you can remind someone else of his or her value in Christ too.

> You are wholly God's own and can find the fullness of your identity in what God has called and created you to be as proclaimed in the Scriptures.

Digging Deeper

God calls us into His family to be His children. But that's not all. He asks us to spread His love to the world, so we can share the story of Christ to everyone we meet. **Read Isaiah 52:7.** Now that we are God's chosen people, what are we called to do? Which of the instructions is most difficult for you?

✤ Personal Challenge

Now that you know how much God loves and cherishes you, share this information with those around you. This week, make a list of three people you want to share the message of Christ's love with—for the first time or as an encouraging word. Schedule a time to Skype, grab a latte, or chat over the phone as you remind them how loved they are by the Creator.

Leader's Guide

Chapter 1: Wholly Forgiven by God

Focus: You are wholly forgiven by God. The slate has been completely wiped clean. Remembering how much God has forgiven you will strengthen you to extend forgiveness to others.

1. Sometimes accepting forgiveness is more difficult than forgiving others. Often we are our harshest critics. Realizing we need forgiveness is difficult to admit. We may never fully comprehend the depth of God's forgiveness, but whether we understand it or not, God deems us worthy to be redeemed—a truth to celebrate and share with others.

2. **Psalm 86:4–5:** "Rejoice the soul of Your servant, for to You, O Lord, I lift up my soul. For You, Lord, *are* good, and ready to forgive, and abundant in mercy to all those who call upon You."

   Psalm 103:8–12: "The LORD *is* merciful and gracious, slow to anger, and abounding in mercy. He will not always strive *with us*, nor will He keep *His anger* forever. He has not dealt with us according to our sins, nor punished us according to our iniquities. For as the heavens are high above the earth, *so* great is His mercy toward those who fear Him; as far as the east is from the west, *so* far has He removed our transgressions from us."

   Isaiah 1:18: "'Come now, and let us reason together,' says the LORD, 'Though your sins are like scarlet, they shall be as white as snow; though they are red like crimson, they shall be as wool.'"

Isaiah 38:17: "But You have lovingly *delivered* my soul from the pit of corruption, for You have cast all my sins behind Your back."

3. Answers will vary. Encourage participants to copy down which verse resonates with them the most and meditate on it this week.

4.

Scripture	Forgiveness is . . .
Psalm 51:9	God **hiding** His face from our sins.
Colossians 2:13	God **makes** us alive together with Him.
Psalm 32:1	God **covering** our sins.
Micah 7:19	God **throwing** our sins into the deepest sea.

5. Encourage participants to share which verse resonates with them. Invite them to share any other verses or stories about forgiveness that are encouraging to them, such as Luke 7:47–48, Colossians 1:13–14, and Matthew 6:14.

6. People will wrong us—even those closest to us. This is inevitable. No matter how deep the hurt or pain, God challenges and asks us to extend forgiveness to others. Often, extending forgiveness can seem impossible. Spend time in prayer as a group asking God for the courage and strength to forgive those we have listed.

7. When we remember how God has forgiven us wholly and fully, we are filled with the courage and strength to forgive those around us. If a perfect God can forgive us for our mistakes—how much more should we forgive those who have wronged us?

8. God counts nothing against us. By becoming the hands and feet of Christ to those around us, we are called to reconcile and forgive others.

Digging Deeper

We can be challenged by the idea to forgive no matter what debt may be owed us. The king represents God—while we may owe Him more than we could ever repay, we are wholly forgiven. However, we often don't forgive others for lesser debts.

Chapter 2: Wondrous Children of God

Focus: You are God's child! As children of God, we have the privilege of knowing God as our Father. We are promised an eternal inheritance, ushered into the family of God, and given abundant promises regarding our future in heaven with Him.

1. Answers will vary. To be a child of God is to be loved perfectly, forgiven wholly, adopted into the body of Christ, favored by the Most High, and considered a co-heir with Christ. Have each participant share a different facet of being one of God's kids with others to expand the definition.

2. Matthew 6:1–7: "Take heed that you do not do your charitable deeds before men, to be seen by them. Otherwise you have no reward from your **Father** in heaven. Therefore, when you do a charitable deed, do not sound a trumpet before you as the hypocrites do in the synagogues and in the streets, that they may have glory from men. Assuredly, I say to you, they have their reward. But when you do a charitable deed, do not let your left hand know what your right hand is doing, that your charitable deed may be in secret; and your **Father** who sees in secret will Himself reward you openly. And when you pray, you shall not be like the hypocrites. For they love to pray standing in the synagogues and on the corners of the streets, that they may be seen by men. Assuredly, I say to you, they have their reward. But you, when you pray, go into your room, and when you have

shut your door, pray to your **Father** who *is* in the secret *place*; and your **Father** who sees in secret will reward you openly. And when you pray, do not use vain repetitions as the heathen *do*. For they think that they will be heard for their many words."

Recognizing God as our Father strengthens our understanding of His love for us. Where earthly parents are imperfect, God the Father is perfect. God the Father fills the gaps our earthly parents create and overwhelms us with His love and grace. Jesus' intimate relationship with God as Father expands our understanding of His teachings.

3. God the Father is the perfect Father. Many people struggle with understanding God as Father. But we need to remember that where earthly parents may have fallen short, God never falls short—His love is perfect and He intimately knows each of us. In our own parenting, marriage, or friendships, God the Father encourages us to love and forgive like He does—wholly and perfectly.

4. God cares so deeply for the birds; how much more does He care for us? Answers will vary, but encourage participants to spend time praying about what holds them back from trusting God with the questions and doubts that the future brings. Remember: God intimately loves His children.

5. **John 14:1–3:** Jesus prepares a place for us in God's house.

   Romans 8:16–17: We are joint heirs with Christ and will be glorified together.

   Galatians 4:4–7: We have been adopted into God's family and receive the Spirit into our hearts. We are no longer slaves, but kids of God.

   Ephesians 1:3–14: We are adopted through Jesus and have redemption, forgiveness of sins, and salvation.

Titus 3:5-7: Justified by grace, we are heirs according to the hope of eternal life.

Answers will vary.

6. From sending an encouraging letter to a missionary to bringing a meal to a family in your church, the opportunities to show kindness to our brothers and sisters in Christ are endless. Encourage each participant to go out of the way to show kindness and appreciation to another child of God this week.

7. **Revelation 7:16-17:** There won't be hunger or thirst. The sun and heat will not strike. The Lamb will lead us to living waters and God will wipe away every tear.

Revelation 14:13: We may rest from our labors.

Revelation 21:4: All tears will be wiped away. No death, no sorrow, no crying, no pain.

Revelation 21:7: We will be the children of God.

8. Answers will vary. Each participant will resonate with various aspects of being a child of God. Becoming God's kid is something to celebrate with others!

Digging Deeper

God desires us to obey Him in everything—from the smallest tasks and conversations to the big decisions of our lives. God desires the best for His children and will guide us in the path He has marked out.

Chapter 3: Handpicked by God

Focus: You are hand-selected by God! God chose you before the foundation of the world to know Him and bring Him glory through your life. No detail escapes His notice.

1. God can reveal these truths to us by a passage we read in Scripture, in a Sunday sermon, through a conversation with a friend over lattes, or through repetitive lessons we're learning in life. God deeply desires for us to understand that we are known and loved by Him.

2. Through what seems to be chance or a coincidence, God may be trying to get your attention or reveal something to you. God often orchestrates what seem to be chance encounters or conversations.

3. **John 15:16:** God chose and appointed us to bear fruit, not the other way around.

   2 Thessalonians 2:13–15: God chose us from the beginning to be saved. He called us so we may share in the glory of Christ.

   1 Peter 2:9–10: We are a chosen people and God's possession. We are called to declare praises of Him.

4. God knows when we sit and when we rise. He knows our thoughts, our path, where we lie down, and all our ways. He knows our words before they're even on our tongue, and He hems us together. Answers will vary.

5. When the bad times of life roll in, we often seem out of God's reach. We can't help but wonder, "Where are You, God?"

6. Answers will vary. No matter what the circumstance is, we are tempted to forget God's presence and hand on our life.

7. Nothing we do can separate us from God's love. No matter what you or others don't like about your personality, strengths, or weaknesses, God delights in you—His child.

8. Answers will vary. Encourage participants to share the most difficult and the easiest quality listed above.

Digging Deeper

Often when life seems hopeless or when we are stuck at a crossroads, believing God has a plan for us becomes hard. However, when we look back on the valleys and mountaintops over the last several years, we can see God's fingerprints all over our lives. God does have a plan and purpose for us; we need only trust and follow His direction.

Chapter 4: Dear Friend of God

Focus: Just like Abraham, we are invited to journey through the highs and lows of life with God by our side. God offers ultimate friendship and desires to grow in greater intimacy with us day by day.

1. Our BFF is someone we catch up with often, grab coffee with just because, and desire to be around and be like. God is our friend because we desire to speak to Him, listen to Him, and be in His presence.

2. Encourage participants to share mountaintop and valley experiences in their walk with the Lord. As a leader, set the tone and intimacy level by sharing your stories first.

3. In friendship, if you don't speak for a while, the friendship seems to drift. In the same way, if we don't find ourselves actively trying to connect with, talk to, listen to, and hang out with God, our friendship with Him will

begin to drift. For some, it may be that you can't see, hear, or touch God physically.

4. A servant does not know what his master is doing, but a friend has the inside scoop on the plans of God. We may often feel as though we are more like servants, unaware of what God is doing. Yet God invites us to be His friend—making known to us His plans for us and the world.

5. Just as time and practice cultivate a healthy friendship, spiritual disciplines offer specific ways for us to grow in intimacy with Christ. This list is not complete. Spend time considering other spiritual disciplines you can practice this week to develop your friendship with God.

6. **John 11:5:** Jesus loved Martha, her sister, and Lazarus.

   John 11:28–35: Jesus wept over Lazarus's death.

   John 13:23: Jesus loved His disciple.

   John 21:1–9: Jesus provided a meal for His disciples.

7. Answers may include busyness, distraction, lack of discipline, or lack of desire, among others.

8. Cultivating a vibrant relationship with God takes sacrifices such as time, energy, and resources.

Digging Deeper

The Lord spoke to Moses face-to-face, as one speaks to a friend. Moses boldly approached and spoke to God. We can also speak to God and approach Him with boldness as we would a friend.

Chapter 5: Much Beloved of God

Focus: God's love is unconditional and endless. He relentlessly and passionately loves you—His beloved.

1. Whether from a parent, significant other, sibling, or friend, the words "I love you" express the vibrancy of being fully known despite any flaws or shortcomings. When we feel loved, we are more capable of expressing love toward others.

2. The idea of being perfectly and wholly loved by God can escape some. Often, falling into the trap of believing we are not worthy of God's love is easy. Truth is, God loves you endlessly—and His love never fails.

3. Past experiences, a lack of self-confidence, or a misunderstanding of God's love can prevent us from truly experiencing and basking in the love of God.

4. Isaiah 43:1 reads: "But now, thus says the LORD, who created you, [your name], and He who formed you, [your name]: 'Fear not, for I have redeemed you; I have called *you* by your name; You *are* Mine.'" Often, personalizing Scripture turns passages from distant to personal. This isn't only a promise to a distant people, but a promise the Lord extends to us today.

5. **Psalm 108:4:** "For Your mercy *is* great above the heavens, and Your truth *reaches* to the clouds."

   Joel 2:13: "For He *is* gracious and merciful, slow to anger, and of great kindness."

   Isaiah 54:10: "My kindness shall not depart from you."

   Romans 8:32: "He who did not spare His own Son, but delivered Him up for us all."

6. Remind participants that the Hebrew word for "love" in much of the Old Testament can be translated as loving-kindness, mercy, or compassion. We are called to walk in love, just as Christ did and gave Himself up for us. When confronting children, spouses, friends, strangers, or co-workers, we may struggle to show love. In those difficult situations, we can be reminded that Jesus is the ultimate example of perfect love—everything we do should model after Him.

7. Someone walking like Christ is without hypocrisy, hates what is evil, clings to what is good, is diligent, honors others, is zealous, rejoices in hope, is patient in tribulation, remains steadfast in prayer, shares, serves, is hospitable, blesses others, rejoices with others, mourns with others, is of the same mind toward everyone, isn't proud, is not conceited, doesn't repay evil for evil, does right in the eyes of everything, lives at peace with everyone, doesn't take revenge, takes care of his or her enemies, and overcomes evil with good.

8. Answers will vary. Encourage participants to focus on one of the three they listed over the next week and learn to love more like Christ every day.

Digging Deeper

Answers will vary for each person, but loving through words is often easier than loving through our actions. Challenge each participant to not only speak love this week but also walk in love.

Chapter 6: Abundantly Blessed by God

Focus: God longs to bless you and abundantly bless others through you.

1. Often we can let God's blessings and gifts slip by unnoticed and unappreciated. However, when we take a step back and really see how God is moving and working in our lives, the results are unmistakable. God goes to great lengths to love and care for us—His children.

2. When we take the time to see God's fingerprints on our lives in the form of blessings, we are often surprised at all of the events, people, and circumstances divinely appointed as blessings.

3. When we remember and recognize the blessings of God in our lives, an attitude of gratitude, joy, peace, patience, and love naturally come about. As we acknowledge God's work in our lives, we are more at peace and willing to submit every area to God with joy.

4. The Lord promised to make Abraham into a great nation, to bless him, to make his name great, for him to become a blessing, to bless others, to curse others, and that everyone on earth will be blessed through Abraham. The purpose of Abraham's blessing was for all the people on earth to be blessed through him (verse 3).

5. Believing God's blessing is something given to you is an easy place to stop. However, God blesses in order that we may bless others around us.

6. The Israelites were told to gather enough manna for what they needed— their daily bread. If they tried to hoard extra or save some for later, it rotted. Rather than depend on themselves and gather enough for days to come, the Israelites were forced to rely on God's provision and blessing in their lives.

7. Whether a gift or a talent God may have blessed us with, if we aren't using it, we're wasting it. From singing and crafting to speaking and counseling, our blessings were intended to be used for His glory.

8. God provides us with blessings each day to be discovered and shared.

Digging Deeper

Answers will vary. When we obey God's commands, He desires to bless us. However, when we don't walk in God's commands, we don't receive those blessings.

Chapter 7: You Are New, New, New

Focus: With God, nothing is beyond His healing, redemption, transformation, or change—including you! You can live without regret.

1. Answers will vary, but many of the regrets offered in the introduction may be new or challenging to participants. If their biggest regret doesn't exist on the list, encourage participants to share what regrets they wrestle with.

2. Answers will vary. Encourage participants to take the promise of 2 Corinthians 5:17 to heart—we are new, new, new! We don't have to dwell on the past mistakes, but can hold tight to God's promise to restore and keep restoring.

3. This passage reminds us there is no need to dwell on the past because God is making all things new—nothing is impossible for Him.

4. God's plans for His children are much greater than we can imagine. Even if His plan doesn't seem evident today, rest assured that God is doing new things in our lives each and every day.

5. The author of Lamentations shifted from wailing in the sorrows and trials to trusting in God's faithfulness and mercies. God is doing a new work not only in us but in all those around us. Spend time celebrating the work God is doing in others today.

6. God is the Potter molding us into pots of clay for a specific purpose.

7. God may be making each of us new through friendships, work changes, trials, and many other areas. Encourage each participant to share how God is currently working in her life.

8. Answers will vary.

Digging Deeper

Jesus transformed the lives of the man with leprosy, the priest who witnessed the man with leprosy's transformation, the centurion, the centurion's servant, Jesus' followers who witnessed the miracle, Peter, Peter's mother-in-law, and those spirit-possessed. Jesus brought healing and restoration to those who came to Him—transforming their lives forever.

Chapter 8: You Are God's Masterpiece

Focus: You are God's masterpiece—and He is working in and through you in ways more spectacular than you can imagine.

1. We often undertake big projects—knitting, scrapbooking, organizing a 5K race, or a charity benefit. When we see these develop from ideas or dreams into reality, we are witnessing transformation. The same transformation happens in our lives and the lives of those around us through the plans God has for us.

2. Ephesians 2:10: "For we are His workmanship, created in Christ Jesus for good works, which God prepared beforehand that we should walk in them."

3. God's workmanship or poem is also found in creation. Because God is the Creator, His works and attributes are displayed in the wonder of all God has made. The passage suggests the world is full of God's poetic works. The heavens declare the glory of God.

4. Saul was a persecutor of Christians and the church. He approved Stephen's death. He sought to throw into prison anyone who believed in Christ.

5. Saul was transformed by encountering Jesus Christ. Often our encounters with God and difficult times won't look as dramatic as Saul's, but they provide an opportunity to grow and recognize God in areas we didn't see Him before.

6. Paul now preached the good news of Jesus Christ with power and fearlessness. People were astonished at his words. He used his skills as a thinker and debater to prove Jesus was the Messiah. As a result, the church grew and was strengthened during this time.

7. Paul described his transformation from chief sinner to someone who shared the good news of Jesus with the world.

8. Consider the areas of stubbornness, lack of patience, addition, issues within relationships, and financial struggles that need God's transformative power and work.

Digging Deeper

God does not leave things half-finished, but works until completion. In the same way, the work He has begun in us will be completed. This may be hard to believe, but God is true and faithful to His promises.

Chapter 9: You Are Part of God's Big Family

Focus: Through our relationships with others who are God's children, we will grow into all God has created us to be.

1. Use this question as an icebreaker to discuss the story of Derek Redmond and our need for relationship.

2. Answers will vary.

3. Sometimes we can find ourselves wondering if the gifts and talents we have been given matter. Paul takes the time to remind us that no matter what our role, it's significant and important. God wants to use us with the unique talents and gifts He's entrusted us with.

4. Sometimes we can fall prey to thinking our role, function, or talent is more important or essential than others. We may not set out to compare ourselves to others, but when we do, sometimes we can fall into pride. Paul reminds us in 1 Corinthians that each gift is a crucial part of the body of Christ that relies on the other parts of the body.

5. Encourage participants in their God-given gifts and provide hope for those who are still determining their gifts. Remember that we often need other people to help us identify the gifts God has given us. Challenge them to take part in the Personal Challenge of this week's lesson or consider taking a spiritual gifts analysis as a group. Remind participants that the gifts in 1 Corinthians 12 and Romans 12 are representative, not exhaustive.

6. Gently remind participants that it is okay if participants don't know who Paul, Barnabas, or Timothy is in their life, and encourage them to find a mentor, friend, or mentee to fill those roles. Spend time in prayer asking God to bless the people who are pouring into you.

7. The idea of discipleship extends beyond our own desires and needs. We are called to disciple others. These answers may be the same as the above question, but understanding the significance of being poured into and pouring into others is important. Spend time in prayer asking God to bless the people you are pouring into.

8. Encourage participants to think out of the box and express God's love to friends, strangers, or enemies.

Digging Deeper

Before we know who Jesus is, we are strangers and foreigners to God's family. When we accept Christ as Lord, we are welcomed with open arms to God's big family and treated as part of the household. Sometimes we need to be intentional about getting plugged into God's family by becoming more involved in church, joining a small group or Bible study, or looking for specific ways to serve on an ongoing basis within a group of believers.

Chapter 10: You Are Connected

Focus: As a follower of Jesus, you are in Christ and given full access to God around the clock.

---

1. As with any relationship, we may feel close to God one day and distant the next. We may be fueled for Christ and feel closest to God after a weekend retreat, Sunday sermon, or personal devotional time.

2. The everyday tasks of duties and deadlines start piling up and our distance from God may tend to feel greater.

3. Answers will vary. Some participants may love the ability to see all of the creatures roam the earth or join in and name each of the creepy, crawly, furry, scaly animals. While we can't know all of the conversations that took place before the forbidden fruit was eaten, we can imagine Adam and Eve's intimacy with God was something to be celebrated.

4. God did not withdraw from Adam and the woman after they ate the fruit. He pursued them. He still met them and called out to them. God asked, "Where are you?" (verse 8), not to push humankind away but to draw them near. Though God cursed the serpent and the land, He never cursed Adam and the woman. But they still faced ramifications for their disobedience. Eve received her name after the Fall, and God created clothes for them. Being removed from the garden was actually a gift of grace—so they didn't live forever in their knowledge of good and evil.

5. God has called us into fellowship with His Son, Jesus Christ. We may answer this call by spending time in daily devotionals, joining a church body, or serving in some capacity to be Jesus' hands and feet to the world.

6. Abiding in Christ includes remaining in and being rooted in God's love. When we abide in Christ's love, everything we do—our fruits—will be

evidence. Answers will vary. Encourage participants to share what activities or seasons draw them closer to abiding in Christ and which pull them further from accomplishing this.

7. God's Word is useful in any situation for wisdom, guidance, encouragement, or simply falling deeper in love with God. Ask participants to share where the Scripture has been important in their lives.

8. To connect to God we need to cut back our schedules. Rather than saying yes to every opportunity that comes, prayerfully consider where you need to say no to further a healthy relationship with God. Challenge each participant to spend at least ten minutes each day with God—through prayer, Scripture, or listening to a sermon.

Digging Deeper

The Israelites responded through shouts of joy or through weeping. The older people in the crowd who had seen the former temple were the criers—they may have been reminded of the struggles they endured. This is a good reminder that how we respond to God develops and changes over the years.

Chapter 11: You Are an Overcomer

Focus: With God, you can overcome anything. You are more than a conqueror through Jesus Christ.

1. Use this question as an icebreaker to engage participants. Spend time sharing about the rough moments in life and the role God has played even in the toughest of times.

2.

Piece of Armor	Purpose
Belt	Truth
Breastplate	Righteousness
Foot Armor	Preparation of the gospel of peace
Shield	Faith to quench the fiery darts of the wicked one
Helmet	Salvation
Sword	The Word of God

3. Answers will vary. We may feel comfortable using the Word of God (sword), but our faith can become shaky (shield). We may feel comfortable walking in peace (foot armor), but find it difficult to living in righteousness (breastplate).

4. We are to rejoice. We are to walk in gentleness, be anxious for nothing, and pray continually. We are also to fix our minds on that which is noble, just, lovely, of good report, and praiseworthy. And we are to practice contentment in every situation.

5. Practicing each of these helps us cultivate and nourish a healthy, vibrant relationship with God and others. When we walk in gentleness, spend time in prayer, and fix our hope on God, we can't help but be overcomers.

6. The saints in Revelation triumphed through the blood of Christ and the word of their testimony.

7. Remind the participants about the importance of being able to keep their testimonies concise. If time allows, encourage each participant to share their testimony in three minutes or less. Sharing and listening to testimonies is a tribute to how God is moving in our lives and in the lives of those around us.

8. Absolutely nothing can get in between us and the love of God. Spend time brainstorming more ways God has given you the strength, power, and grace to be an overcomer—through confidence, Jesus, friendships, Scripture, courage, a job—the list is endless.

Digging Deeper

Paul seemed to welcome hardship for the sake of the gospel. When we shift our focus from the present and visible to the eternal and invisible, we see that our life is not our own. God uses each of us with specific purposes in mind—to shine for His glory and further the kingdom.

Chapter 12: You Are Wholly God's Own

Focus: You are wholly God's own and can find the fullness of your identity in what God has called and created you to be as proclaimed in the Scriptures.

1. Encourage participants to spend time in prayer expressing their gratitude for the truths revealed in those passages.

2. God may be echoing truths about each of us through books, sermons, conversations, or Scripture.

3. Encourage each participant to copy down the passage she most struggles to remember and memorize it over the upcoming week.

4. No matter what we assume God's attitude is toward us, knowing above all else God delights in us, His children, is important. He desires to lavish us with His unending love.

5. Answers will vary, but rarely do we find our worth and value from Scripture and God. Often, our value comes from the media or those around us.

6. Reflecting on these truths will affect how we view ourselves, God, and others. When we are deemed worthy, our self-esteem rubs off on our daily lives, our relationship with God, and how we treat others who are deemed worthy and valuable as well.

7. Answers will vary. Leave time to share each participant's response during your time together.

8. Write out the list of passages from the chapter, meditate on Scripture, or be intentional about reminding each other about our identity as God's beloved children each day.

Digging Deeper

Isaiah said that the feet of those who bring good news (the gospel), proclaim peace, bring good tidings, and proclaim salvation are beautiful. Spend time this week meditating on this passage. Ask God for the courage and boldness to enact this in your life starting now.

Notes

Chapter Seven

1. www.guardian.co.uk/lifeandstyle/2012/feb/01/top-five-regrets-of-the-dying.

Chapter Nine

1. http://sports.espn.go.com/espn/espn25/story?page=moments/94.

Chapter Eleven

1. www.gordon.edu/article.cfm?iArticleID=878&iReferrerPageID=1676&iPrevCatl D=134&bLive=1.

About the Author

Margaret Feinberg (www.margaretfeinberg.com) is a popular Bible teacher and speaker at churches and leading conferences such as Catalyst, Thrive, and Extraordinary Women. Her books and Bible studies have sold more than 600,000 copies and received critical acclaim and extensive national media coverage from CNN, the Associated Press, *USA Today*, *The Los Angeles Times*, *The Washington Post*, and more.

She was recently named one of the 50 Women shaping church and culture by *Christianity Today*, one of the 30 Voices who will help lead the church in the next decade by *Charisma* magazine, and one of the "40 Under 40" who will shape Christian publishing by *Christian Retailing* magazine. Margaret currently lives in Colorado with her husband, Leif, and their superpup, Hershey. One of her favorite treats is hearing from her readers, so connect with her on Facebook or Twitter @mafeinberg or drop her a note through her website.

About the Author